Global Issues

Racism

Clive Gifford

GLOBAL ISSUES

DRUGS   EQUAL OPPORTUNITIES   RACISM   TERRORISM

Visit our website at www.whitecap.ca.

Library and Archives Canada Cataloguing in Publication

Gifford, Clive
        Racism / Clive Gifford.
(Global Issues)
Includes index

ISBN 1-55285-745-X

    1. Racism--Juvenile literature. I. Title. II. Series: Global issues (North Vancouver, B.C.).

HT1521.G53 2006   j305.8   C2005-905644-4

Editor: Clare Weaver
Editorial Manager: Joyce Bentley
Designer: Mark Whitchurch
Consultant: John Polley
Picture Researcher: Isabel Swanson

The Publisher acknowledges the financial support of the Government of Canada through the Book Publishing Industry Development Program for our publishing activities.

Printed and bound in China
10 9 8 7 6 5 4 3 2 1

Picture Acknowledgements
We wish to thank the following individuals and organizations for their help and assistance, and for supplying material in their collections: AKG London 8, 13, 16; Alamy 20; Associated Press 5 middle, 32; Britkid 37; Corbis 4 (Tom and Dee Ann McCarthy), 19 (Annie Griffiths), 46 (John Henley); David Hoffman Photography 28, 29, 33; John Birdsall Photography 10, 43; Mary Evans Picture Library 14, 17 (Steve Rumney); NASA 36; Panos Pictures 18 (Stephen Dupont); Popperfoto 3, (Reuters), 5 top (Fabrizio Bensch/Reuters), 24, 25, 26, 47 (Reuters); Rex Features 1 (Tom Kidd), 5 bottom, 6 (Kim Ludbrook), 7 (Erik Pendzich), 11 (Julian Andrews), 21, 22, 23 (Slanther/PNS), 27 (Richard Oliver), 30 (Rankin), 31 (Sipa), 34 (Tom Kidd), 38 (Robert W Kelley/Timepix), 39, 41 (Sipa), 42, 44 (Roland Schiager), 45 (Action Press); Science Photo Library 9 (Nelson Max/LLNL/Peter Arnold Inc); Topham Picturepoint *front cover*, 15, 35 (ANP), 40 (Pressnet). Artwork by Michael Posen. The pictures used in this book do not show the actual people named in the case studies in the text.

CONTENTS

Errol's Story

Errol is a 17-year-old African American who experienced racism in several parts of the US before his family's latest move to New York. He hopes to attend college to study medicine.

"I ALWAYS REMEMBER name-calling and monkey signs made at me and the other black kids out of class. My mother told me not to let it get to me. "To react back makes you as low as them," she told me, and I tried, but it still made me feel bad about myself, like I wasn't as good as them.

When we moved west, I went from being one of many black kids to the only one in the neighborhood. People, parents, kids, old people; they all used to stare at me. Several times, folks told me stores were closed even when I could see others inside buying things. When I went into stores, I was followed around by clerks, like I was gonna steal something. I thought it was funny the first time. But it happened all the time.

School was bad there. I tried to make friends, but one kid, Ryan, got beaten up by older white kids for hanging out with me and stopped. My grades got worse and some of the teachers started to pick on me for making noise in class when it couldn't be me—I had no one to talk to. My locker was broken into and "Nigger thief" written inside but I hadn't stolen anything. I don't want to say much about the worst thing that happened. Some white men I didn't know grabbed me one night and tied me up. They hit my legs with a metal pipe over and over again. I needed three operations on my right leg. At the time, I thought I was going to die.

We moved to New York right after that. I hear about lots of crime here, but I feel much safer, like I'm not the one guy everyone wants to hate anymore. I still don't understand how you hate people who are strangers you know nothing about. I still have nightmares about what happened. I never want to be like them."

Problems in other areas

Errol is just one of the many victims of racism found all over the world.

EUROPE
In Europe, membership of racist groups is growing and the number of racist attacks is also on the increase. In Germany, attacks increased by 40 percent in 2000.

SOUTH AFRICA
From 1948 for over 40 years, the apartheid system kept black and white people apart. Despite making much progress in the 1990s, South Africa still suffers from racial discrimination and racist attacks.

AUSTRALIA
Although they have lived in Australia for 50,000 years, Aborigines were only granted full citizenship rights in 1967. Before 1971, anyone considered more than half Aboriginal was excluded from the population figures.

What Is Racism?

"Racism has been to human relationships what cancer has been to human existence. It is a disease that eats away at the very fabric of humanity itself."
Oscar Peterson, black jazz pianist

There are over six billion people living on Earth in more than 200 countries with thousands of different beliefs and elements of culture. Most people celebrate the differences between peoples because they add richness and diversity to life. Some use certain differences to single out groups as inferior and deserving of unfair treatment. Racism is one such way of singling people out. It has caused misery and suffering for millions.

A demonstration against the British National Party draws different antiracist groups together, including the Anti-Nazi League.

RACISM IS BASED on the flawed belief that a person's character and abilities are determined by the racial group to which they are thought to belong, and that certain racial groups are inferior to others. To determine which racial group a person belongs to, racist people look purely at a person's physical appearance; not at what kind of personality, interests, or beliefs they have. Racism doesn't focus on all aspects of physical appearance, but mainly on skin color and, sometimes, certain facial features.

People who believe in racism are called racists. Racists believe that their own race, or racial group, is superior to other groups. The "higher race" is seen as more creative, intelligent, and morally stronger. Other "lesser races" are considered not to be trustworthy, well-behaved, hardworking, or bright. As a result, racists feel justified in treating members of other groups as inferiors.

This idea of superior and inferior racial groups has been used as an excuse for the most horrific actions, from preventing another race from studying or seeking employment to beatings, murders, and even attempts to wipe out an entire race.

The term racism is sometimes widely used and applied to any group that attacks or discriminates against another group. This book concentrates on a more strict definition put forward by some experts: the racism as developed and practiced by Europeans and people of European origin. As John McKenzie, founder of the Recovering Racists Network says, "I do feel that racism requires 'prejudice combined with power' and believe that whites in North America and Europe are in a unique position to have the power to turn their prejudice into racism."

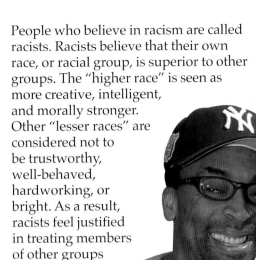

"When you're told every day for four hundred years that you're subhuman, when you rob people of self-worth, knowledge, and history, there's nothing worse you can do."

Spike Lee, African American filmmaker

Spike Lee is a successful African American filmmaker. He has often addressed race and racism in the modern United States through his films.

How many races are there?

Race is the idea that the people of the world can be separated into distinct groups. These groups, or races, are biologically different to each other and can be identified through skin color, facial appearance, and their character and skills. Racists use this idea to label certain races as fundamentally different and inferior. One of the founders of race theory, the Frenchman Count Joseph-Arthur Gobineau (1816–82), said there were three races—white, black, and yellow. Others divided the world's population into as many as 30 different races. In all cases, these races were seen as completely different species or subspecies of human beings.

Science has since shown there is just one species of people to which we all belong, and that people of all colors and appearances have a similar potential. In 1945, the United Nations Economic, Scientific and Cultural Organization (UNESCO) stated that "available scientific evidence provides no basis for believing that the groups of mankind differ in their innate capacity for intellectual and emotional development."

Count Joseph-Arthur Gobineau was a French diplomat, writer, and social thinker of the 1800s. He believed in the white race's superiority over others and felt that the more a civilization became mixed racially, the more it lost its creativity and value.

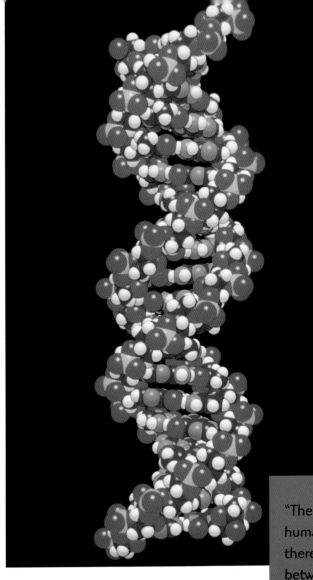

A computer model of a strand of DNA with different colored spheres representing different kinds of atoms. Research into DNA has helped disprove the notion that there are different biological races.

"The biological concept of race amongst humans is meaningless. It implies that there are sharp genetic differences between populations. The concept of 'race' is essentially a political concept, and as it is applied, a racist concept."

Source: CARF Issue 32, June 1996

Modern research into genetics has revealed how people differ from each other. Around 30,000 genes control a person's physical characteristics. These create the great variety of shapes, sizes, and looks that make the world's six billion people different from each other. Yet only around six genes control all the differences in skin color. This means that people of different skin colors can have many more genes in common than people of the same skin color do. There are no distinct sets of black or white genes. The idea of different biological races of people is false.

Why is race still an issue?

Despite the notion of race being proven wrong by science, race remains a huge issue. This is because many people still believe in the idea of widely different races and because many societies continue to give "racial" differences a great amount of significance.

Black and white men murdered for fighting racism

Lin Newborn was black, Daniel Shersty was white. Both were members of Anti-Racist Action. Both were murdered in Las Vegas in July 1998. John Butler, the leader of a racist group, the Independent Nazi Skins, was found guilty of the twin killing.

Source: Las Vegas Review Journal

Is hating Jews or the French racist?

No. While racists use race to distinguish between different peoples, there are other ways in which groups can be singled out. Some people define themselves and others by the religions they hold and, instead of embracing and respecting a range of beliefs, act against peoples of other religions. Other people take pride in their country to extremes, believing their nation to be superior and peoples of other countries inferior. Being xenophobic (hating and fearing foreign peoples) or intolerant of other religions is not the same as racism, although they can be just as harmful.

One of the many thousands of happy mixed race families in the United Kingdom.

A participator in the Notting Hill Carnival in London, England in August, 2002. The Notting Hill Carnival is one of many carnivals, festivals, and events, which enliven the culture of the United Kingdom.

Does ethnic mean racial?

No. Ethnicity is the cultural beliefs and lifestyle of a group of people that set them apart from others. Different things can distinguish a particular ethnic group, but common ones are language, history, religion, and styles of dress. Ethnic differences are learned, whereas a person is born with the color of their skin.

I'm white, so does racism affect me?

Racism's direct victims are mainly nonwhite people, but white anti-racism campaigners are frequently the victims of racist action. The whites in mixed black and white families are often singled out by racists for "betraying their own race." In some places, merely having a black or Asian friend has been enough for a white person to receive hate mail, letter-bombs, or bricks through home windows. Racism in an area can create a climate of mistrust and fear, which can envelop everyone who lives there, not just the racists and their direct victims.

DEBATE—Do different beliefs equal different peoples?

* Yes. If people believe in different things and live in different ways, then surely they are different.
* No. Ethnic differences such as beliefs, dress, and diet are not a biological part of a person. People from one ethnic group can learn and practice the ways of other ethnic groups.

When Did Racism Start?

Racism has its roots in the age of European colonialism, which began over 400 years ago. As Europeans discovered and claimed overseas lands as colonies, the belief grew that European civilization was the greatest the world had ever known. Europeans thus felt justified in treating other peoples as inferior.

FROM THE 1500s and on, many European countries like France, Portugal, Spain, Holland, and Great Britain explored and claimed lands in Africa, Asia, the Americas, and the Pacific as their own. Little attempt was made by the arriving colonists to understand the civilization, culture, and beliefs of the native peoples. Instead, they were often thought of as savages, primitives, and, in some cases, no better than animals. As a result, the colonists assumed the right to take their lands, ruling them without agreement, and killing, mistreating, and enslaving millions of people.

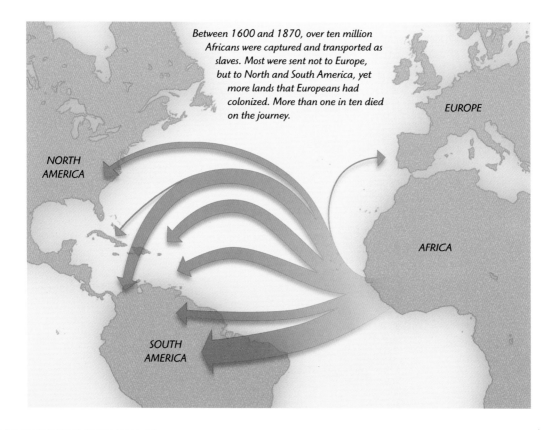

Between 1600 and 1870, over ten million Africans were captured and transported as slaves. Most were sent not to Europe, but to North and South America, yet more lands that Europeans had colonized. More than one in ten died on the journey.

NORTH AMERICA

EUROPE

AFRICA

SOUTH AMERICA

Seventeenth-century views of race

"I am apt to suspect the Negroes, and in general, all other species of men, to be naturally inferior to the whites. There never was any civilized nation of any other complection [complexion] than white."

David Hume (1711–76), Scottish philosopher and historian

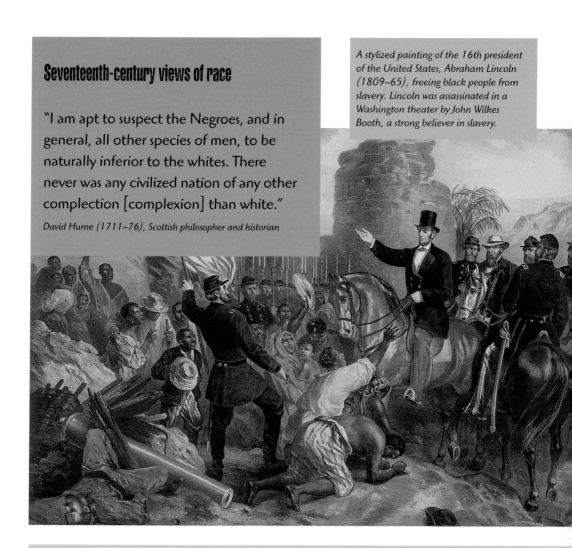

A stylized painting of the 16th president of the United States, Abraham Lincoln (1809–65), freeing black people from slavery. Lincoln was assassinated in a Washington theater by John Wilkes Booth, a strong believer in slavery.

DEBATE—Were sixteenth- to nineteenth-century Europeans better as they had the most advanced civilization?

- Yes. The European nations had built amazing structures and made great advances in science, the arts, and exploration. They were the most advanced civilization in the world, meaning they were better than other civilizations, which had created less.
- No. Who is to judge whether a civilization is advanced or not? For example, Australian Aborigines may not have built large buildings, but they lived in harmony with their land in ways white people are learning from today. Why should the successes of a civilization make them superior to other peoples?

How did racism alter as an idea?

Race was first used to describe a person's family background—who their ancestors were, for example. It was also sometimes used when talking about the country a person lived in or the religion they practiced, with phrases such as the "the Jewish race" or "the French are the finest race." In the 1700s came the idea that people and other creatures were of one kind of fixed race, which never changed. Mixed-race people were thought of as exceptions in nature who would die out quickly.

In the 1800s, the naturalist Charles Darwin wrote about the idea of evolution and how different species of creatures change and adapt over time to where they live. Instead of exploding the myth of races of people that never change, parts of Darwin's work were seized upon by some people to promote and justify the idea that white Europeans were superior to all others. For example, some took his concept of "survival of the fittest" and maintained that, because the white race was most advanced, it rightly exploited other, less advanced races. Others took Darwin's idea of evolution and maintained that they could measure skulls and other physical features to place all races in a line back to our monkey ancestors. White peoples were the most evolved and advanced and black peoples the least evolved and closest to the monkeys.

These ideas were held by many people until the mid-1900s, when science showed that distinct species of humans do not exist and the world learned of the Nazis' attempt at genocide (the deliberate killing of an entire people).

In the 1800s, many anthropologists believed that measuring skulls could be used as a way of defining racial types.

In Mein Kampf (My Struggle), published in 1925, Adolf Hitler maintained that it was the Nazi Party's duty "to promote the victory of the better and stronger [races] and demand the subordination of the inferior and weaker."

What is anti-Semitism?

Anti-Semitism is the hatred of Jews, which has led to Jews being persecuted for their beliefs in different countries for many centuries. There is no such thing as a Jewish race—Judaism is a religion—but in Nazi Germany (1933–45), the Jewish people were treated as a race. Under the leadership of Adolf Hitler, the Nazis believed in racial types with the white German, or Aryan, race being supreme and the Jews cast as the biggest threat to Aryan supremacy. The Jewish *Untermenschen* (meaning "subhumans"),

were first harassed and then persecuted ruthlessly. By 1941, the Nazis' attempt to exterminate all Jewish people was under way. By the end of World War II, four years later, six million of Europe's eight million Jews had been murdered.

A world shocked at the Nazi genocide formed the United Nations in 1945 with the aim "to save succeeding generations from the scourge of war." Although racism continued to exist, it became more and more discredited as a way of acting publicly.

How Does Racism Affect People?

Racism can affect people in many different ways. At its most common, racism involves distressing comments, jokes, and stereotypes. It can also prevent people from receiving fair access to jobs, education, and justice. At its most extreme, racism can lead to violence, murder, and entire countries or regions where different races live apart.

Family moves after racist attacks

Femi Olayisade, a member of the Nigerian royal family who works for Christian Aid in Northern Ireland, has said he has been forced out of his home after a series of racist attacks. His windows have been smashed three times in the last month; each attack was more violent. "I've never had any quarrel with anybody around here," he said. "People just want to make life uncomfortable for me because I'm black."

Source: BBC News, May, 2002

In the film In the Heat of the Night, *Sidney Poitier played a black detective who was initially discriminated against by a prejudiced white officer, played by Rod Steiger. The film was controversial at the time (1967), as it was one of the first Hollywood movies to feature a black actor in the lead.*

This cartoon, dating from 1895, depicts dancing black children conforming to the racial stereotype of the time.

REJUDICE MEANS TO make up your mind about someone or something before holding all the facts—it literally means to prejudge. Prejudice is based on ignorance and usually involves a negative judgement or conclusion being made against a person, group, or idea before knowing what that person, group, or idea is really like. A prejudiced person is likely to hold on to their views even when presented with the truth. Racially prejudiced people believe they know the character and attributes of people of color just because they can see their skin color.

What is stereotyping?

Much racial prejudice is based on stereotypes. A stereotype is a fixed idea about what people are like. It tends to reduce whole groups of people to one characteristic—for example, all Mexicans are lazy or all Irish people are drunks. Even when the characteristic appears positive, such as "all African Americans are good athletes," stereotypes are still insulting because they label and group together millions of people without thinking of them as individuals.

Racial stereotyping has occurred in all kinds of media including television, movies, and children's books. African American men, for example, have been frequently portrayed as slow-witted and only good at physical work. In crime movies, they were found on both good and bad sides, but until recently, often only as lowly henchmen taking orders from white bosses. Stereotyping in the media has been damaging because it limits how a person sees others and themselves, and helps to reinforce people's prejudices.

American study finds high levels of stereotyping remain

A study by the National Opinion Research Center (NORC) found that more than half of those surveyed rated African Americans as less intelligent than whites. Sixty-two percent rated African Americans as lazier than whites.

Source: NORC

DEBATE—Should old books that are now considered racist be kept in public libraries?

- Yes. As a record of what society once was like, it is important that people have access to them. Banning books like these gives them more publicity than they deserve.
- No. They are demeaning and offensive to racial groups, and may inspire certain people to adopt racist attitudes.

Are language and racism connected?

Spoken and written language can be used to cause offence. There are many obvious racist names, such as calling a black person "darkie," that are used in this way.

Other terms help reinforce stereotypes and may be used through ignorance, often with no spite intended. For example, many people in the United States refer to all hispanic people as immigrants—people who were born elsewhere before settling in the US. However, many hispanics were born in the United States.

Australian Aboriginal children playing in a run-down street in the major city of Sydney. This deprived neighborhood is just a five-minute drive from the grandeur of the world-famous Sydney Opera House.

What is racial discrimination?

Discrimination involves treating one group less favorably than another. Racial discrimination denies members of one racial group access to opportunities open to others: for example, when a college refuses entry to a black student with higher than average grades, then admits a white student with poorer grades. Racial discrimination has hit many people of color extremely hard by reducing or denying their access to the basic essentials of life, such as education, jobs, and housing.

A 1989 study of employment agencies in Canada found that 94 percent admitted to discriminating against job seekers on the basis of skin color. In New Zealand, Maoris are three to four times more likely than whites to be unemployed. It is the same for Aborigines in Australia and only a little better for black people in many European countries. This only reinforces stereotypes and prejudice that certain racial groups are less likely to make good employees. People in jobs can also be discriminated against by being passed over for promotion, or by being given less favorable work conditions than their white co-workers.

These female students are celebrating their graduation from Howard University. Their future is bright compared to those African Americans who are discriminated against and fail to get a university education.

What Is Racial Harassment?

Racial harassment involves racially motivated verbal abuse or physical violence against a person or their property. Racial harassment is very common in many countries and has proven to be hard to stamp out.

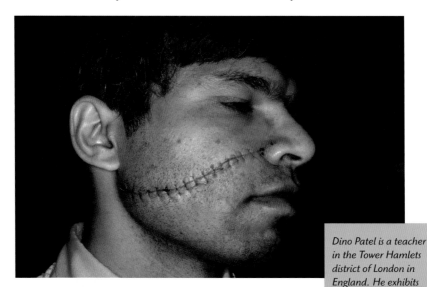

Dino Patel is a teacher in the Tower Hamlets district of London in England. He exhibits the horrific results of a racist attack, which occurred outside an antiracist concert.

Racist murder

Alberto Adriano did not have a chance. A German citizen, of Mozambican origin, he was kicked to death on the streets of the eastern German city of Dessau by racist attackers in 2000. They stripped him naked and screamed "nigger pig" and "this is the march of the German resistance" as they kicked his head with steel-tipped boots. In August, his attackers were jailed for murder. His wife was too scared to attend the trial and remained under police protection.

Source: Yojana Sharma, Interpress Service, December, 2000

RACIAL HARASSMENT ranges from racist comments, jokes, and graffiti to arson (deliberate burning of houses or other property), violent attacks, and, as in the case of Alberto Adriano (see panel on left) and others, murder. In the UK, for example, there are an estimated 110,000 recorded instances of racial harassment every year. Many thousands more occur but go unreported.

These cemetery graves have been vandalized by Nazi sympathisers who have used aerosol paints to spray the Nazi symbol known as a swastika.

DEBATE—Are racist jokes just having some fun?

- Yes. People make fun of those who wear glasses or are overweight. It's just having some fun and people should learn to have be able to laugh at themselves.
- No. They trivialize racism, which has caused much human misery. They act as a way of promoting racial prejudice and damaging racial stereotypes.

Racial harassment at home, school, and work is often thought to be trivial, involving name-calling, racist jokes, petty theft, and vandalism. However, it is often persistent and repeated week-in, week-out for a long period of time. This becomes incredibly distressing for its victims, shattering their confidence and leaving them feeling isolated, frightened, lonely, and an unwanted part of the community. This feeling of alienation can be increased when neighbors, classmates, and co-workers do nothing to stop it and offer little support.

"I had a teacher who in front of the class used to call me 'swamp woman' because I came from the West Indies. That was supposed to be a big joke. But I didn't think it was so funny. People saying you lived in shacks ... or calling you 'coconut heads' and 'monkey chasers.'"

Margaret Prescod-Roberts on living in New York as a schoolgirl.

What is institutional racism?

Just as individuals can be racist, so can institutions. The institution can be a business, a government, or an individual agency of a government such as the court system or the police force. Institutional racism can occur whether the members of the institution are racist or not. Its processes (way of doing things) are what lead to racial discrimination and, in some cases, racial harassment.

Rodney King

In March, 1991, African American Rodney King was stopped by four white police officers in Los Angeles who then severely beat him as he lay on the ground. The incident was captured on video and the officers were arrested, but an all-white jury found them not guilty the following year. The verdict sparked major riots in which over 50 people died.

Are the police racist?

"Negroes [black people] deserve to be hit first, then asked their name." These aren't the words of a slave owner from the 1700s, but the advice given in 1999 by a senior Austrian police officer while he was training 30 junior officers. Austria is far from alone. Police forces all over the world have been accused both of institutional racism and of protecting racist members of their forces. In South Africa, there have been a number of instances of white police officers ignoring white racist attacks on black people. In many countries, police target nonwhite people as suspects much more than whites—an action sometimes called racial profiling. In the US, African Americans are much more likely than whites to be stopped and searched by the police. Although many white police officers the world over are determinedly antiracist, some police are racist or operate within a force where institutional racism occurs.

A still from the video depicting Rodney King being beaten while lying on the ground.

AMATEUR VIDEO

MAR. 3 1991

Why are so many nonwhites in prison?

In most countries with a white majority, nonwhite people make up more of the prison population than their proportion in society. For example, African Americans comprise 12.7 percent of the total US population, but over 45 percent of those in prison. Some people feel that this is because nonwhites are simply less trustworthy and prone to crime. Others think that in unequal societies with racial discrimination, nonwhites are more likely to be poor and unemployed, and that these conditions tend to breed crime. A third point of view is that many nonwhite prisoners are victims of institutional racism in the police and legal system. This sees them investigated and brought to justice more vigorously than whites, handed longer or more frequent prison sentences, and, in some cases, falsely accused and convicted of crimes.

A heavy British police presence at the Inquiry into the murder of Stephen Lawrence. This black British teenager, who wanted to be an architect, was stabbed to death by a group of white youths in southeast London in 1993. Nobody was convicted of his murder and the Inquiry found many failings in the police investigation.

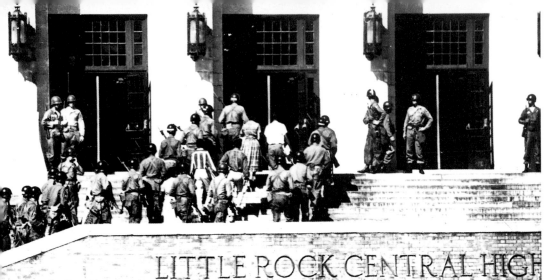

LITTLE ROCK CENTRAL HIGH

What is segregation?

Segregation is the keeping apart of different races in some, or all, areas of everyday life. It is large-scale institutional racism and has involved separate schools, housing, transportation, and other facilities for different races.

Three former segregation laws in US states

Books shall not be interchangeable between the white and colored schools, but shall continue to be used by the race first using them. *North Carolina*

No colored barber shall serve as a barber [to] white women or girls. *Georgia*

It shall be unlawful for a negro and white person to play together or in company with each other at any game of pool or billiards. *Alabama*

Segregation has rarely been performed with equality between whites and nonwhites in mind. In 1896, the Supreme Court ruled that "separate but equal" facilities were allowable by law. This decision helped to justify racial discrimination and segregation throughout much of the US, especially the southern states, for over 60 years. The "Jim Crow" laws (named after a black minstrel character) insisted on separate hotels, seating areas, restrooms, and schools. Facilities for African Americans were frequently of poorer quality than those for whites. Only a few African Americans were able to attend college, and racial discrimination was practiced openly in employment. Tests to register for elections were often applied dishonestly, preventing many nonwhites from voting. There was also a difference in the quality of justice and protection from the law granted to African Americans and white people. Thousands of crimes against African Americans, including hundreds of murders by white gangs or mobs (lynchings), went unpunished.

An African American hanged by a white lynch mob in the state of Georgia. Thousands of African Americans were killed in this way in the late 1800s and early 1900s, often without any proof of guilt for committing a crime.

When did US segregation end?

It wasn't until a decade after World War II that segregation started to be challenged successfully. A series of events in the 1950s, including protests, court decisions against segregated schooling, and the murder of a 14-year-old black boy, Emmet Till, whose "crime" was greeting a white woman, sparked changes. The campaign for integration (an end to segregation) grew throughout the 1950s and 60s, during which time segregation was challenged in court and by high-profile protests and, in many areas, removed.

Historic Supreme Court Ruling against segregated schooling

"To separate them from others of similar age and qualifications solely because of their race generates a feeling of inferiority as to their status in the community that may affect their hearts and minds in a way unlikely ever to be undone. We conclude that in the field of public education the doctrine of 'separate but equal' has no place."

Source: US Supreme Court Ruling in the case of Brown vs Board of Education of Topeka, 1954

What Was Apartheid?

Designed to protect the interests of a white minority, segregation became a country-wide policy in South Africa under the leadership of Daniel F. Malan. It was called the policy of apartheid, which literally means "apartness."

SOUTH AFRICA WAS already a racially divided country with some laws separating blacks from whites before apartheid started officially in 1948. Apartheid's laws forced everyone suspected of not being of European origin to be classified by race. Every aspect of life was segregated by race. There was whites-only public transportation, leisure facilities, beaches, and even park benches. The Mixed Marriages Act made it illegal to marry someone of a different race to yourself, while the Group Areas Act forced people of certain races to live in specific areas. Many black people were forced to live in townships outside major cities or in "homelands" in rural areas. In these designated areas, the farmland, schooling, healthcare, and job opportunities were extremely poor. Many blacks were forced to work for white employers with their pay, conditions, and rights vastly inferior to those of white workers.

Movement between areas, and civil rights, were strictly controlled by the authorities. Laws gave the police and military sweeping powers to put down any resistance to the apartheid regime. On many occasions, the white authorities acted brutally. In 1960, a demonstration

Some of the dead and wounded victims of the Sharpeville massacre in 1960.

South Africa's leader explains need for apartheid

"Apartheid is a way of saving the white civilization from vanishing beneath the black sea of South Africa's non-European populations."

National Party leader, Dr. Daniel F. Malan, 1948

Victim's mother confronts death squad leader

Maria Ntuli's son, Jeremiah, disappeared in 1986. It turned out that he was one of about ten young black men kidnapped and put into a van by a notorious white "death squad" that operated around the city of Pretoria. The van was filled with explosives and then pushed over a cliff. When confronted by Ntuli over the loss of her son, Brigadier Jack Cronje, leader of the death squads replied, "I thought I was doing the right thing."

Source: "Facing The Truth," PBS TV

against apartheid in the black township of Sharpeville resulted in the police opening fire, killing 69 men, women, and children and injuring over 180 more. Resistance to apartheid also came from outside South Africa with protests, condemnation by the United Nations, sanctions, and boycotts. Sanctions banned certain economic trade occurring between South Africa and other countries. Boycotts prevented South Africa from taking part in many international sporting and cultural events. It wasn't until the late 1980s and early 1990s that apartheid's grip on South African society was loosened.

Segregation in action, as seen at a beach for whites only in the Cape region of South Africa.

Why Do People Become Racist?

It is sometimes thought that only poor and uneducated people are racists. The truth is that racists come from all walks of life, including those who are wealthy, have a university education, or are in positions of power and responsibility. No one is born racist. It is something that is learned. How do people become racist?

This British National Party rally called in 1991 celebrated the racist killing of a young black teenager, Rolan Adams.

IN THE PAST, people thought that children simply adopted similar attitudes to their parents and other family members. If adults or older children in a family were prejudiced, used racist language, and racially discriminated and harassed, then the child would follow. Today, research has shown that the way in which people become racist is more complex. Prejudiced attitudes in a family are just one factor. Some racists may not come from racist families but had unhappy childhoods where fear and violence were common. Others may feel alone and aggressive. Many become bullies. Hitting out verbally and physically, they seek an easy target—a person with a skin color different to theirs. Other children and teenagers may be influenced by their friends or join a gang whose members have racist attitudes. Many young people desperately want to fit in and start adopting similar attitudes as the rest of their gang or peer group.

Are older people more racist?

There is no simple answer. Some people find their racist views are changed by their experiences as they get older and they turn their back on racism. Others become more fearful of crime and resentful of nonwhite immigrants coming to their country. These fears are often played upon by racist organizations who, in meetings and their literature, distort black crime figures, portray nonwhite groups as more criminal, and highlight nonwhite immigrants "stealing" white people's welfare benefits.

A member of the former National Front hands out literature in London. Many racist groups attempt to spread their message via leaflets, books, and posters.

What is scapegoating?

Many racist groups use a technique called scapegoating to promote racist beliefs. When there are problems in a society or area, such as poverty, unemployment, poor quality housing, and crime, people naturally want to blame someone or something. Scapegoating is wrongly blaming a group of people for problems in society. Scapegoating often appeals to those who feel that most political parties have failed them and who feel powerless to do anything about their own situation. It is convenient and tempting to many to make scapegoats out of people who look physically different. Racist groups use the anger that many people feel when they are poor, unemployed, or feel they are

not getting their fair share. They twist facts and figures to show that everything would be different and much better if it weren't for the presence of a racial group in their society. The British National Party (BNP), for example, recently won many election votes in poor towns in England. They made Southeast Asians the scapegoats for going to the front of housing and welfare lines and replacing churches in the area with mosques. In Australia, the party against immigration for nonwhites received 25 percent of the vote in Queensland. Its leader, Pauline Hanson, believes that a multiracial society could never unite and that immigrants and Aborigines are getting more benefits than white Australians.

Pauline Hanson was the founder of the anti-immigration One Nation political party in Australia. This party brought race issues to the forefront of Australian politics.

A group of people claiming asylum while living in an old hanger, the site of a Red Cross center in Sangatte, northern France.

Are asylum seekers being scapegoated?

In the past 15 years, refugees and asylum seekers (those seeking refugee status) have become a big political issue in Europe and Australia. The numbers granted refugee status are relatively small, measured in hundreds, or sometimes thousands, in most countries. This fact doesn't stop racist groups from claiming the country will be flooded or swamped by needy foreign people who will take from society and contribute nothing back. Asylum seekers make easy targets for scapegoating by racist groups. Many fled their home country leaving their wealth and possessions behind. They may not be familiar with the language, customs, or practices of the country they are in and need assistance. This leads to resentment that they are "butting in line" for help. Many asylum seekers may have been attacked, tortured, and seen their families and friends die. Yet, if they are not granted refugee status, they are labeled as "bogus" and accused of trying to cheat the system.

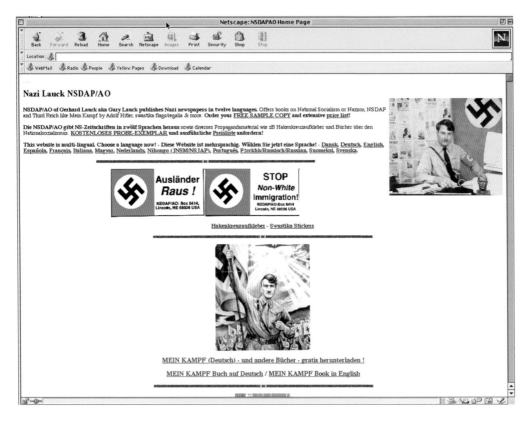

The homepage of a German neo-Nazi site on the World Wide Web. In the year 2000, Germany outlawed web addresses with Nazi slogans in its own country, but it can do little about websites with Nazi and racist content based in other parts of the world.

How do racist groups recruit members?

Racist groups use many different ways to obtain new members. Some groups cloak their more extreme racist beliefs by promoting themselves as decent citizens concerned about religion or political issues. Getting their views across in books, leaflets, and at meetings and rallies, they hope to influence people to become more prejudiced and to recruit more members. Other groups seek out impressionable and violent-minded people through the Internet, racist rock concerts, at sport events, and in bars. They attempt to make violence against nonwhites seem glamorous and exciting in an attempt to get people to join their "gang."

Former member recalls the lure of joining the British National Party

"It was dangerous and exciting... They were good to me. I belonged, I felt included, part of it... I felt untouchable. A lot of the people involved had unhappy childhoods... not much hope. In the group, we felt empowered with family spirit."

Matthew Collins
Source: British newspaper, The Observer, March, 2002

Racist groups have become more sophisticated in their recruitment methods and are targeting white teenagers who are still forming their opinions. They try to appeal to this age group through their favorite forms of media and entertainment, including computer games, websites, and rock music. An organization against racism and anti-Semitism, the Anti-Defamation League, has cataloged over 500 racist rock bands, many in the US, UK, Germany, Italy, Poland, and Sweden. Using the Internet is a cheap and efficient way for racist groups to promote their beliefs to a wide audience, including children and teenagers. Racist websites have flourished in the last ten years. According to the Simon Wiesenthal Center, there was just one website in 1995 promoting racial hatred. By the middle of 1999, that figure had risen to over 2,100.

Resistance Records release racist computer game

Ethnic Cleansing, a CD-ROM "shoot 'em up" game has been released by a record company owned by the National Alliance, the largest and most active neo-Nazi organization in the US. The player, who can dress as a member of the Ku Klux Klan or as a skinhead, roams the streets murdering "predatory subhumans"—African Americans, Jews, and Hispanics—to save the white world. This ultraviolent game features many racist messages, and monkey sounds are made when African Americans are killed.

Warhammer are a British pro-Nazi band promoting race hate through song lyrics and titles such as "Die Jew Die" and "This is England—Get Out."

What racist organizations are there?

No one knows precisely how many racist groups exist worldwide as some work in secret while others are loose-knit groups, which split and reform over time. What is known is that they exist in number in all countries where there is a white majority, and in some countries where white people are a minority as well. Many racist groups aim purely to stir up racial hatred among whites and promote violence, harassment, and discrimination. Others try to rewrite history, denying that the Nazis performed atrocities and blaming the media for bias. A number of racist organizations have moved into politics, contesting elections and seeking to win publicity and, ultimately, political power. In the UK, for example, the British National Party doubled its membership and captured local council seats between 1998 and 2002.

Should we worry about racist parties?

Some people think that all the media attention given to racist political parties is damaging and out of proportion to their success. They argue that in most countries with a white majority, far-right parties have never gained overall power and win very few seats in parliaments or assemblies. By highlighting their election "successes," the media gives them more publicity with which they can air their views.

Others point to what they believe is an alarming rise in the number of votes for racist political parties in France, Germany, Belgium, Holland, and the UK. In Austria, the far-right Freedom Party, under the leadership of Jorg Haider, won 27 percent of the vote in the 1999 general election. As a result, they took many senior government posts. In many countries, dissatisfaction with the

Members of the Ku Klux Klan in their distinctive clothing, hoods, and insignia pose in front of their notorious symbol of terror—a burning cross.

Dutch right-wing politician, Pym Fortuyn, shown months before his assassination in 2002. Following Fortuyn's death, the party of which he was leader, the LPF, became the second largest in the Netherlands.

mainstream political parties is at an all-time high. Millions of people feel that the major parties have let them down and are not speaking for them. Some of these voters are turning to a radical, racist alternative.

What does the KKK stand for?

KKK is the abbreviation of one of the most infamous racist organizations of all, the Ku Klux Klan. Formed in 1866, the KKK was based in the South. It grew in power until, at its peak in the 1920s, it may have had as many as five million members. The KKK targeted African Americans, Catholics, and Jewish people with terrifying violence. The power of the KKK has diminished, but many ex-Klan members remain active, forming their own groups and still promoting racism.

Ex-Ku Klux Klan member in court

Dennis M. McGiffen, a former Ku Klux Klan grand wizard, faces up to 15 years in prison after pleading guilty to firearms conspiracy and possession charges. McGiffen, 35, of Wood River, Illinois, and four other men were charged in an alleged plot to blow up the Southern Poverty Law Center and the Anti-Defamation League in New York, and assassinate civil rights leader Morris Dees.

Source: Terrorism in the US: 1998 (FBI report)

How Is Racism Tackled?

Racism occurs in many forms, and there are equally as many ways to tackle it. Across the world, there are hundreds of organizations, large and small, and thousands of individuals, all looking to combat racism and its effects.

MOST RACISM IS founded on prejudice which itself is based on ignorance of other people. Racial awareness seeks to spread information about how all peoples are from the same race, and also how to understand and respect differences in history, culture, and lifestyle. Books, videos, CD-ROMs, and classroom activities, along with public, school, and workplace events, are all used to promote tolerance and understanding to help eliminate racial prejudice.

Why is breaking stereotypes important?

Breaking stereotypes challenges lazy and prejudiced images of peoples and helps to promote the idea that people of all racial groups can be as successful as each other. It can also provide racial minorities with proof that success can be achieved even against the odds in a discriminating society. Early breakthroughs can provide a springboard for more to follow. For example, in 1978, Viv Anderson—at the time, one of only a handful of black professional soccer players in the UK—became the first to play for England's national team. Twenty years later, around 15 percent of all professional soccer players in Britain are black. In sports, arts, and entertainment fields where nonwhite people have excelled, they can become heroes and role models not just for nonwhite, but for white people as well. This helps to break down prejudice further, but there is still much work to be done, and many organizations campaign to break stereotypes. For example, the stereotype of Japanese being too small and weak to play professional soccer still exists in much of Europe, while in 2000, out of a total 11,000 university professors in the UK, only 29 were black and 179 Asian.

In 1992, Mae C. Jemison became the first African American woman to travel into space. Her mission aboard the space shuttle Endeavor was to conduct experiments on the effects of zero gravity on people and animals.

Playing out racist situations

A class in a Manchester, England school produced a play in response to a white classmate's racist taunting of a black girl. The play has since been shown to the whole school and to local police forces. The ten-year-old boy said, "I don't know why I started being racist, really. Sometimes people get on my nerves and I get a lot of anger in me and it's hard to keep it in. We've learned that you pay the consequences for being racist, and you shouldn't be racist because it hurts people's feelings inside and outside. It's only skin color—that's all. If I saw people being racist, I would say stop it because I know what it's like now."

Source: British television program, "Newsround," BBC TV

Educational websites that explore and discuss issues about race and identity are extremely important in countering racism. This is the homepage of the Britkid website, which seeks to educate people about the different cultures found in the United Kingdom.

The Reverend Martin Luther King Jr arm-in-arm with white church leader, Eugene Carson Blake, on a 1963 rally in Washington DC.

I.U.E.
AFL-CIO
FOR
FULL
EMPLOYMENT

WE MARCH FOR JOBS FOR ALL NOW!

FIRST BAPTIST CHURCH

Are civil protests ever successful?

Although protests and campaigns can fail, and sometimes lead to violence, a number have contributed to lasting, positive change. This was the case in the US, with the civil rights movement pioneered by organizations such as the National Association for the Advancement of Colored People (NAACP) and the Congress Of Racial Equality (CORE) and individuals such as Dr. Martin Luther King, Jr. Growing from the 1950s on, the civil rights movement used largely nonviolent tactics, such as boycotts of certain services, powerful speeches, mass marches, and demonstrations. They achieved changes in law and society leading to more equal treatment for African Americans. Other protests and campaigns have also led to some success. For example, after National Front leader Jean Marie Le Pen's strong first-round showing in the 2002 French Presidential elections, large protests against his racist policies were held. These helped to publicize his racist stance, leading to a reduction of his vote in the final election.

Who are the targets of campaigns?

There are many different targets for the large range of campaigns and protests that occur every year. Many campaigns seek to challenge and influence governments to change laws or to ask institutions, such as local councils and the police, to enforce laws more fairly. Other protests and campaigns are aimed at society in general, to make public a particular issue, such as cases of racial discrimination or severe cases of racial harassment. Some protests and campaigns target racists and racist groups by monitoring and highlighting their activities. Sometimes, there are direct protests outside meetings of racist groups. Other initiatives call for censorship to prevent racists from communicating their ideas through speeches, images, actions, or literature.

In Germany, it is against the law to buy new copies of Hitler's book Mein Kampf, wear Nazi clothing and symbols, or publish pro-Nazi books or leaflets. Many politicians in Germany have also called for a violent racist group, the NPD, to be prevented from holding rallies and demonstrations, but others are concerned about limiting people's rights, such as their freedom to speak and hold meetings.

How can racists be considered victims?

Some consider racists themselves to be victims of their own ignorance and prejudice, and of the persuasive methods used to recruit and keep people in racist groups. Racial awareness education has been aimed at children who have repeatedly made racist comments, and at young adults found guilty of racial harassment offences. Some organizations try to assist adults wanting to leave extreme racist groups, a move that can be both difficult and dangerous. In Sweden, a government-backed initiative called Exit has helped more than 80 people to leave neo-Nazi groups safely and return to peaceful society.

Kleines
Juden-
Brevier

Adolf Hitler
Zitate

DEBATE—Should racist speakers be denied a platform and censored?

- Yes. Racist views should not be tolerated in a civilized society. Racist speeches can generate hatred and violence and are offensive to the majority of people in a country.

- No. It is the basic right of every person to have the freedom to speak their opinion, however unpleasant the majority of a society find their views. Sometimes such views are agreed with by a large proportion of a population.

Do laws really combat racism?

Dr. Martin Luther King, Jr. once said, "Judicial decrees may not change the heart, but they can restrain the heartless." By this, he meant that laws cannot remove prejudice; they can only make actions based on prejudice illegal. Laws have seen many nonwhite people in North America, Australasia, South Africa, and Europe benefit from the outlawing of racial violence, harassment, and discrimination. Yet, without education and ways of fighting prejudice, the problem of racism will remain, even if it is driven underground.

Some antiracist laws have set up special bodies to help promote and enforce them. For example, in the UK, the Race Relations Act of 1976 set up the Commission for Racial Equality (CRE), which offers advice and support for victims of racial discrimination.

What are equal opportunities?

Equal opportunities are policies, usually backed by laws, designed to counter discrimination against certain groups. In a fair society, religion, sex, or skin color should have no bearing on the jobs, education, and other services a person is selected for or offered. This is the basis behind equal opportunities policies found in a number of countries. Although they have helped to remove some racial discrimination, equal opportunities schemes can sometimes be hard to police. It is difficult to prove that a person was rejected because of his or her skin color when a prejudiced employer or official gives other reasons for not hiring or admitting them.

Pop singer and former member of the Spice Girls, Mel B, is depicted as a white woman in an advertisement by the UK's Commission for Racial Equality (CRE), designed to show how skin color does not equal a person's character, personality, and abilities.

World Conference Against Racism, Racial Discrimination, Xenophobia and Related Intolerance
Conférence mondiale contre le racisme, la discrimination raciale, la xénophobie et l'intolerance qui y est associée
31/08/01 - 07/09/01
DURBAN

The World Conference on Racism opens in the South African city of Durban in 2001. Those in attendance include the Palestinian leader, Yasser Arafat.

"The villains are Mr. and Mrs. Complacent. They either don't understand what racism is and how it needs to be tackled or, in the face of the facts, they deny this is something they have to address."

Gurbux Singh, former Head of the CRE (Commission for Racial Equality) in the UK.

What is positive discrimination?

Positive discrimination, also known as affirmative action, doesn't disregard a person's skin color, sex, or religion. On the contrary, it offers preferential treatment to those groups previously discriminated against. It attempts to compensate for past discrimination by setting goals for more recruitment from minorities and by publicizing opportunities more to minority groups. It can also mean choosing the candidate from a minority group when faced with two or more candidates of equal standing.

DEBATE—Is positive discrimination a good idea?

- Yes. It helps to compensate for the wrongs of the past. Many suitably qualified individuals from minority groups have benefited from positive discrimination policies.
- No. As a form of discrimination, it is unfair. It can also lead to resentment and antagonism in the majority population. Offering everyone an equal chance of success is the only fair policy.

In the UK, Doreen Lawrence campaigned for
an inquiry into the failure to convict the killers of her
teenage son, Stephen.

Community stands up to racism

In April, 2002, residents of a Welsh
town where a Southeast Asian
shopkeeper was racially harassed by a
former member of the Ku Klux Klan
made a stand against racism. At a
public meeting, residents showed
their support for the victims of Alan
Beshella, 52, who was sent to jail after
harassing shopkeeper Mohammed
Nawaz. Mr. Nawaz had planned to
leave the town after the incident,
but later announced that he had
been persuaded to stay in the area
by local people.

Source: BBC News

Do I have to join an organization to help?

No. There are plenty of other ways in
which an individual can counter racism
and its effects. On their own, a person
can seek out information and learn more
about racism and the issues that
surround it. They can inform others of
what they've learned and try to remove
prejudice in their circle of friends. Many
people have learned a lot from speaking
to people who have been victims of
different forms of racism. An individual
can also make a stand against any racist
comments and actions they experience.
Few antiracists think that confronting
such behavior with violence is the
answer, but challenging and reporting
such behavior to teachers and parents
can help. On many occasions, people
find that when they make a stand
against racism, friends, neighbors, co-
workers, and classmates may follow.

Can individuals make a difference?

Sometimes an issue like racism can seem
so big and complex that individuals feel
there is nothing they can do. This is
simply untrue. Many individuals—
from Dr. Martin Luther King, Jr. and
Nelson Mandela to the schoolgirl or boy
who reports racist bullying—have made
an important difference. Every person
can make a contribution to ridding the
world of racism.

Advice when confronted by racism

"Obviously, the way forward isn't violence... The way to solve it is to bite your lip and kind of rise above it. I know it's hard, but it's something that makes you a better person, and you don't want to go down to their level of being ill-mannered and having no self-respect. If you are in the classroom, you tell a teacher as soon as it happens. On a football pitch [soccer field], you let the referee know that something like that has happened."

Soccer player for England's national team, Rio Ferdinand
Source: Red Card To Racism campaign

A wall of portraits painted by children in a British primary school reflect the different peoples they encounter in their everyday life.

Will Racism Ever Disappear?

In many ways, racism should be yesterday's news. Scientists have proven that there are no separate species or subspecies of the human race and that the person you are does not depend on the color of your skin but on your upbringing, environment, and experience. Yet, racism continues to exist in many forms in different parts of the world. Can it ever be overcome?

EVERY DAY BRINGS examples of racism in action. In fact, the numbers of racial harassment cases reported in many European countries have stayed steady or even risen in the last five years. Does this mean that the work of individuals, lobby groups, and governments has been in vain? Not necessarily. Some increases in reported racist actions may be due to improvements in the way information is gathered. For example, publicity drives in many countries have urged victims of racism to come forward with their experiences. Some of these victims are able to receive help. As a result, many people believe that a larger proportion of racist incidents are being reported than in the past.

Despite support in opinion polls falling from their highs of the late 1990s, Jorg Haider's anti-immigration Freedom Party still commands around a fifth of Austria's electoral support.

Has there been any real progress?

Throughout the world, there have been hundreds of small-scale success stories of individuals facing up to their own and their families' racist attitudes and, through education and experience, overcoming them. Using classroom discussions, activities, and antiracist videos and books, thousands of children have turned their back on racist bullying. Knowledge and understanding of different peoples and cultures is increasing through improvements in transportation and communication, and through the breaking of stereotypes through the media, arts and entertainment, and, sometimes, politics.

In 1996, the most influential international organization in the world appointed a new leader. Kofi Annan, from Ghana in west Africa, became the first black Secretary-General of the UN. Four years later, Colin Powell, previously Commander-in-Chief of the US forces, was appointed Secretary of State by the new president George W. Bush. Powell was the first black person to hold this position, considered the most powerful position after the presidency.

Colin Powell's address at the Republican Party National Convention in 2000

"The issue of race still casts a shadow over our society, despite the impressive progress we have made over the last 40 years to overcome this legacy of our troubled past that is still with us."

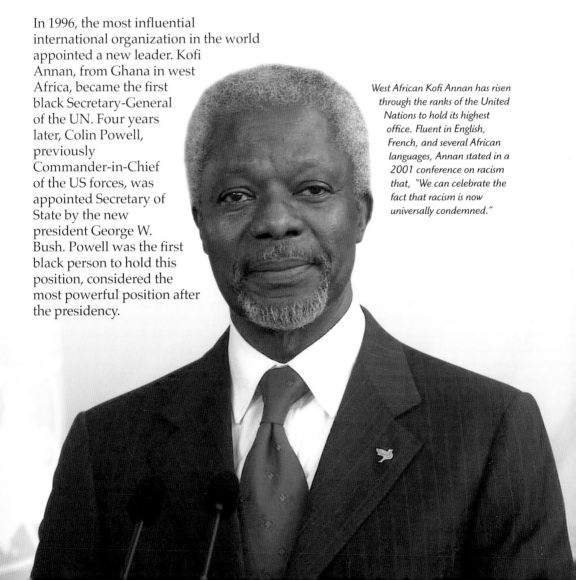

West African Kofi Annan has risen through the ranks of the United Nations to hold its highest office. Fluent in English, French, and several African languages, Annan stated in a 2001 conference on racism that, "We can celebrate the fact that racism is now universally condemned."

Has the fight against racism worked?

Countering all the different ways that racism occurs is an ongoing process, which makes it impossible to label as a success or failure so far. Certainly, some progress has been made, but in many cases, the success has been partial. For example, in the Race UK 2002 survey, 54 percent of white, 57 percent of black, and 52 percent of Southeast Asian respondents felt that Britain is a more tolerant place than it was ten years ago. Yet, 48.5 percent of all those surveyed still thought Britain was a racist society.

The events in South Africa in the 1990s are a nationwide example of a partial success. In April, 1994, after a number of years of dismantling the apartheid policy and structure, black South Africans were able to vote freely in presidential elections for the first time. Nelson Mandela became South Africa's first black president and a major world figure.

Removing the often bitter and violent

legacy of over 40 years of apartheid and many decades more of racial exploitation has proven a slow and painful process. Mandela's successor as president, Thabo Mbeki, stated in 2000 that, "We have not won the struggle against racism." An example of the struggle ahead occurred in June, 2002. The opposition-led Cape Town local government approved the building of a wall separating a mainly wealthy white area from a poorer, black area. An African National Congress (ANC) politician called it "an apartheid Berlin Wall ... appalling, wrong, and immoral."

The hope for a true rainbow nation (see panel on the opposite page), living in harmony, is still some way off, but this doesn't mean that South Africa has failed —more that it has only partially succeeded. There is still much work to be done, and this applies across the entire world. Pressure and support groups cannot do it by themselves. Nor can governments or the United Nations. It

takes the support of ordinary people, all people, to learn about others, to examine their own views and prejudices, to challenge racism where it exists, and to embrace a multiracial world.

Mandela holds out hopes for rainbow nation

"The time for the healing of the wounds has come. The moment to bridge the chasms that divide us has come. The time to build is upon us... We enter into a covenant that we shall build the society in which all South Africans, both black and white, will be able to walk tall, without any fear in their hearts, assured of their inalienable right to human dignity—a rainbow nation at peace with itself and the world."

Source: excerpt from Nelson Mandela's presidential inauguration speech, May 10, 1994

Nelson Mandela presents the 1995 Rugby Union World Cup to the captain of the victorious South African team, Francois Piennar.

A group of children enjoy playing tug-of-war with little thought to the skin color of the participants.

"The world is a painting full of many colors. Let's keep it that way."

Child attending the anti-Le Pen rallies in Paris, May, 2002.
Source: British newspaper, The Guardian

REFERENCE

Different countries collect statistics on racism in different ways, making it hard to make comparisons between countries. In the future, organizations such as the European Racism and Xenophobia Network (RAXEN) hope to build databases of statistics, which are comparable between countries.

HATE CRIMES IN THE UNITED STATES BY CAUSE

Attacks reported to the FBI

Race:	5,514
Religion:	1,720
Sexual Orientation:	1,488
Nationality:	956
Multiple Bias:	17
Disability:	27
Total:	9,722

Source: FBI Hate Crimes, 1998

US STATISTICS FOR AFRICAN AMERICANS

African Americans are:
12.7% of total US population
15% of total drug users
36.8% of those arrested for drugs violations
24% of African Americans 25 and over have not graduated from high school (16% of whites)
26.5% of African Americans live below the poverty line (11% whites)

Source: US Bureau of Justice Statistics 1999, www.prisonactivisit.org

AUSTRALIAN ABORIGINAL SOCIAL CONDITIONS

Percentage Unemployment (2000)
Aborigines 23%
National average 7%

Percentage completing high school (2000)
Aborigines 32%
National average 73%

Percentage in professional jobs (2001)
Aborigines 7%
White 14.2%

Average personal income (1996)
Aboriginal AUS$190 per week
National average AUS$292 per week

Source: UNWCAR, Australian Bureau of Statistics

RACIAL ATTACKS REPORTED TO POLICE IN ENGLAND AND WALES, UK

Year	Attacks
1988:	4,383
1992:	7,734
1993–4:	11,878
1995–6:	12,199
1997–8:	13,878

Source: Commission for Racial Equality, British Crime Survey

EUROPEAN ATTITUDES TO RACE, 2000

Conducted by the European Monitoring Centre on Racism and Xenophobia, the Eurobarometer was a major survey of attitudes to race, religion, and discrimination across many European countries.

Q. Do you personally find the presence of people of another race disturbing in your daily life?

	Yes	No	Don't Know
Austria	14%	79%	7%
Belgium	27%	70%	3%
Denmark	23%	76%	1%
Finland	11%	87%	2%
France	19%	75%	6%
Germany	17%	75%	8%
Greece	24%	73%	3%
Ireland	20%	74%	6%
Italy	14%	82%	4%
Netherlands	10%	88%	2%
Portugal	11%	86%	3%
Sweden	11%	87%	2%
Spain	5%	93%	2%
UK	16%	79%	5%
EU average:	15%	80%	5%

Q. Does a country's diversity in terms of race, religion, and culture add to its strengths?

	Tend To Agree	Tend To Disagree	Don't Know
Austria	47%	33%	20%
Belgium	37%	50%	13%
Denmark	58%	28%	14%
Finland	50%	37%	13%
France	54%	33%	13%
Germany	39%	45%	16%
Greece	22%	69%	9%
Ireland	43%	33%	24%
Italy	41%	39%	20%
Netherlands	53%	33%	14%
Portugal	50%	29%	21%
Sweden	26%	41%	33%
Spain	48%	30%	22%
UK	51%	30%	19%

Source: European Monitoring Centre on Racism and Xenophobia

GLOSSARY

affirmative action Also known as positive discrimination, this is a policy adopted by a country or organization to attempt to make up for previous discrimination by favoring disadvantaged groups.

African Americans Term used in the US to describe black Americans.

alienation The act of making people feel alone, isolated, and afraid.

anthropology The study of human origins, society, and culture.

anti-Semitism The hatred of the Jewish peoples.

apartheid Literally meaning "Apartness," the political policies of the South African government from 1948 until the early 1990s designed to keep peoples segregated based on their color.

asylum A place of safety and refuge usually provided by a country for those seeking refugee status.

boycott The cutting of relations with a country, company, or group of people by removing trade, cultural, and government links.

colony A country ruled by another country as part of its empire.

culture The traditions, values, lifestyles, and beliefs shared by a group of people.

discrimination The act of treating people worse because they belong to a particular group.

ethnic group A group of people who share the same distinct culture, religion, way of life, or language.

fascism A form of government or political philosophy that believes in racism, rule by a dictator, and certain nations being superior to all others.

genetics The scientific study of human characteristics passed down through generations through genes.

genocide The deliberate attempt to kill all of the members of a racial, ethnic, or religious group.

hate crime Crimes of violence, theft, or harassment motivated by the criminal's hatred of a particular racial, religious, or other group.

Hispanic Spanish-speaking people living in the US whose families originally came from Latin America.

human rights The basic rights of all human beings, such as the right to free speech, food, and shelter.

immigrant Someone who moves to and settles in another country.

institutional racism A modern term used to describe the processes inside an organization that can result in racial discrimination regardless of whether or not the members of the organization are racist.

lynching The execution of an accused person by a mob outside of the law.

multiracial Involving people of different racial groups.

nationalism Beliefs that a person's nation is superior to others.

neo- New, modern, or recent. For example, neo-Nazi groups are groups of people holding similar beliefs to the Nazis of the mid-1900s.

persecute To harass, injure, or kill a particular group of people.

positive discrimination See affirmative action.

prejudice Negative feelings or attitudes toward a group of people that are not based on facts.

propaganda The use of the mass media, such as television and newspapers, to influence people's attitudes, often using lies and distortion.

racial profiling Targeting police investigations on the basis of a person's race or national origin.

refugee A person forced to seek refuge away from their homeland because of war or some form of persecution.

scapegoat A person or group wrongly blamed for the problems or deeds of others.

segregation The separation of different racial groups as far as possible in everyday life.

slavery A system where one group of people own another group as their property and force them to work.

stereotype A widely held belief that all members of a particular racial, ethnic, or social group have the same, often negative, characteristics.

xenophobia A fear and hatred of foreigners.

FURTHER INFORMATION

BOOKS

Nobody's Born A Racist
Produced largely by young adults for young adults, this is a constructive guide to fighting racism. Available from: The Students Commission, 70 University Ave., Ste. 1050, Toronto, Ontario M5J 2M4, Canada.

Amnesty International by Deena Tuttle
    (World Almanac Library 2004)
United Nations by Frank Tarsitaus
    (WorldAlmanac Library 2004)
Two titles from a series of books that reveals each organization's mission and major activities, its history, and the structure that lets its vision be played out around the world.

Civil Liberties (Lucent Books 2000)
Ethnic Violence (Lucent Books 1997)
Human Rights (Lucent Books 2003)
Multicultural America (Lucent Books
    2004)
Series of books by various authors that offers an in-depth overview of each topic. Can be used both for reports and for casual, informative reading. Includes photographs, illustrations, and provocative editorial cartoons.

Interracial Relationships (Greenhaven
    Press 2000)
Is Racism a Serious Problem
    (Greenhaven Press 2005)
Reparations for American Slavery
    (Greenhaven Press 2004)
White Supremacy Groups (Greenhaven
    Press 2003)
Slavery Today (Greenhaven Press 2004)
Titles in the *At Issue* series include a wide range of opinions on a single controversial issue. There are opinions from eyewitnesses, scientific journals, government officials and others.

ORGANIZATIONS

EAFORD
The International Organization for the Elimination of All Forms of Racial Discrimination
2025 Eye Street NW, Suite 1120
Washington, D.C. 20006

National Center for Human Rights Education
The mission of the NCHRE is to build a human rights movement in the United States by training community leaders and student activists to apply human rights standards to issues of injustice.
118 East Maple St
Decatur, GA 30030
tel: 678-904-2640
fax: 678-904-2641
email: info@nchre.org

Gustavus Myers Center for the Study of Human Rights in the United States
The Center promotes living out diversity equitably. It encourages and welcomes the increasing range of scholarly and advocacy publications which help deal equitably with pluralism. It encourages collective action to dismantle structures of domination. Now in its 21st year, it believes fervently that in the struggle is the hope.
Loretta J. Williams, Ph.D., Director
Simmons College
300 The Fenway
Boston, Massachusetts 02115
tel: 617-521-2171
email: lorewill@myerscenter.org

International Human Rights Law Group
Global Rights is a human rights advocacy group that partners with local activists to challenge injustice and amplify new voices within the global

discourse. With offices in countries around the world, it helps local activists create just societies through proven strategies for effecting change.
1200 18th Street, N.W., Suite 602
Washington, D.C. 20036
tel: 202-822-4600
fax: 202-822-4606
www.hrlawgroup.org

National Coalition of Students Resisting Racism

A multi-racial coalition of college and university students struggling to dismantle racism on a national level.
2300 N. Ivanhoe Street
Muncie, IN 47304

Southern Regional Council

An organization promoting racial justice and human rights in the south of the United States and beyond.
133 Carnegie Way N.W., Suite 900
Atlanta, GA 30303-1031
email: info@southerncouncil.org

Canadian Race Relations Foundation (CRRF)

4576 Yonge Street, Suite 701
Toronto, Ontario M2N 6N4
Canada
Email: info@crr.ca

Alliance for Justice

The Alliance for Justice is a US national association of environmental, civil rights, mental health, women's, children's and consumer advocacy organizations.
11 Dupont Circle, NW, 2nd Floor,
Washington, DC 20036
tel: (202) 822 6070,
fax: (202) 822 6068
email: alliance@afj.org

American Civil Liberties Union

The ACLU continues to pursue the release of information about detainee torture and abuse.
125 Broad Street, 18th Floor
New York, NY 10004
www.aclu.org

Citizens' Commission on Civil Rights

The CCCR is an organization established in 1982 to monitor the civil rights policies and practices of the US federal government. Its work is grounded in the belief that the civil rights agenda benefits the entire country, not just particular interest groups.
www.cccr.org

National Association for the Advancement of Colored People

The primary focus of the NAACP continues to be the protection and enhancement of the civil rights of African Americans and other minorities.
NAACP National Headquarters
4805 Mt. Hope Drive
Baltimore Maryland 21215
tel: Toll Free: (877) NAACP-98
NAACP 24 Hour Hotline (410) 521-4939
www.naacp.org

National Congress of American Indians

Since 1944, the National Congress of American Indians has been working to inform the public and Congress on the governmental rights of American Indians and Alaska Natives.
1301 Connecticut Ave NW, Suite 200
Washington D.C. 20036
tel: (202) 466-7767
fax: (202) 466-7797
email: ncai@ncai.org

National Association for the Advancement of Colored People
The primary focus of the NAACP continues to be the protection and enhancement of the civil rights of African Americans and other minorities.
NAACP National Headquarters
4805 Mt. Hope Drive
Baltimore Maryland 21215
tel: Toll Free: (877) NAACP-98
NAACP 24 Hour Hotline (410) 521-4939
www.naacp.org

National Congress of American Indians
Since 1944, the National Congress of American Indians has been working to inform the public and Congress on the governmental rights of American Indians and Alaska Natives.
1301 Connecticut Ave NW, Suite 200
Washington D.C. 20036
tel: (202) 466-7767
fax: (202) 466-7797
email: ncai@ncai.org

Martin Luther King, Jr Memorial Foundation
Martin Luther King, Jr. National Memorial Project
Foundation, Inc.
401 F Street, NW, Suite 334
Washington, DC 20001
tel: 888-484-3373

WEBSITES
www.un.org/WCAR
The starting point for a comprehensive website dealing with the details of the United Nations World Conference Against Racism, held in Johannesburg, South Africa, in 2001, and the issues and news raised since.

www.amnesty.org
Home of Amnesty International, the human rights charitable organization, this website features a library of documents including reports and information on racism.

www.vrx.net/aar
The homepage of the Artists Against Racism initiative with features, links, and recommended books and events.

www.crr.ca
The Canadian Race Relations Foundation's webpages with reports and factsheets downloadable from the site.

www.hrw.org/refugees
The webpages of Human Rights Watch, an organization dedicated to observing the human rights conditions of peoples all over the world.

www.antiracismnet.org
AntiRacism.net's site providing articles and resources for antiracism supporters.

www.eburg.com/beyond.prejudice
A multimedia project informing and advising on reducing prejudice.

www.racismnoway.com.au
Australian website aimed at schools, explaining racism and how to recognize it. The site contains lesson plans, factsheets, a timeline, and news.

www.icare.to
The Internet Centre Anti-Racism Europe (I CARE) was founded by a number of groups to coordinate information in the battle against racism.

www.united.non-profit.nl
Based in the Netherlands, UNITED for Intercultural Action is a European network of over 500 organizations seeking to halt racism.

www.arc.org
The webpages of ERASE (Expose Racism & Advance School Excellence), this site offers resources for students and teachers as well as a quiz section and reports.

www.fair.org/racism-desk
The starting point for the Racism Watch Desk, of FAIR, an American media watch group that details and comments on the media's misrepresentation of nonwhite people.

www.erace.com
An interesting site with history, resource links, and videos from this American foundation promoting racial harmony.

www.carf.demon.co.uk
The home on the Internet of the UK's Campaign Against Racism & Fascism, which produces an independent magazine online with news, reports of incidents, and campaigns.

www.sahrc.org.za
The website of South Africa's Human Rights Commission, set up in 1995.

www.imadr.org
The website of the International Movement Against All Forms of Discrimination and Racism, an organization based in Japan and Switzerland.

http://motlc.wiesenthal.com/
Sponsored by the Simon Wiesenthal Center, the Museum of Tolerance contains many resources and features on the Holocaust and anti-Semitism.

www.innercity.org/holt
A detailed timeline with articles, images, and tables chronicling slavery in the U.S. from 1619 up to today.

INDEX